Nubia

SKETCHES, NOTES AND PHOTOGRAPHS

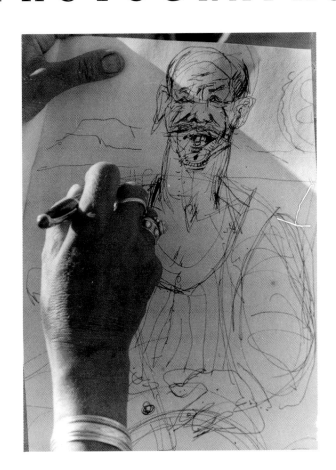

Margo Veillon

SCORPION PUBLISHING LTD
LONDON

First published in 1994 by
Scorpion Publishing Ltd
Victoria House
Victoria Road
Buckhurst Hill
Essex
England

ISBN 0 905906 71 3

Editor: Leonard Harrow
Design: Zena Flax

Typeset by MasterType, Newport, Essex
Printed and bound in Singapore by Craft Print

Contents

Acknowledgements

I would like to thank the following for their support in the preparation of this book

Mrs Chantal Bastien
Mrs Alma Culik
Mr B A Gent and his son, Kent, England
Dr Gibson, Dean AUC
Mrs Beate Herzberg
Mrs Hohmeyer
Dr and Mrs Myliani
Professor Tadeus Reichstein
Mr Gordon Rouquette
Margaret Seay, Singapore
Mrs Edgar Seeholzer
Mr Jean Claude Veillon
Mr François Veillon, Basle

Photographs by Georg Gerster: pages 3, 8, 13, 137

Introduction

Margo Veillon was born on 19 February 1907 in the Abbasiyyah district of Cairo, the second child and only daughter of a Swiss businessman and his Austrian wife, both of whom had artistic and musical interests. While she was still an infant the family moved to Maydan Tawfiqiyyah near the centre of the city, where she spent most of her childhood, drawing 'monsters' at the age of seven, beginning to paint at the age of nine, learning at fourteen (from her cousin Lily Humm) how to convey the idea of a cat in motion, making cut-outs at sixteen. A zealous student only of art, she was sent to no fewer that six schools in Cairo – five different primary schools and the Lycée Français – and finally two schools in Switzerland.

In 1923 the family moved to a villa in Ma'adi, eleven kilometres south of Cairo. Surrounded by a wide belt of desert and agricultural land, this residential suburb was then a small garden development less than twenty years old. Zoned and regulated to restrain over-building, it was traversed by a tree-lined irrigation canal and neighboured by mud-built agricultural villages and bedouin settlements, which offered splendid subjects for sketching and painting. Margo Veillon has maintained a residence in Ma'adi ever since. In 1953 she built her own house and studio, where she continues to spend the months from October to June.

When Margo Veillon returned to Egypt from school in Zurich in 1924, she had already decided to become a professional artist. To broaden her skills, she enrolled in the Accademia Scarselli, a private Italian-owned art school, the best the city had to offer. She was then seventeen. After a year of uninspiring instruction she struck out for herself, relying thenceforth mainly upon her own sense of direction and her taste for experiment, but also upon the advice and example of other artists. In 1928 she participated for the first time in the annual Salon du Caire. Over the next decades she was to acquire the technical mastery of oil painting, tempera, gouache, pastel, etching, engraving, mosaic and ceramics, that is obvious in her work, while becoming an occasional sculptor and a formidable photographer.

In 1926, the year before her father's death, she spent a few weeks in Paris, where she bought the first of many books she was to own about the work of a painter she had hardly heard of before, Picasso, heavily illustrated with drawings from the Negro and Analytical Cubist periods. In 1929, however, Margo Veillon was invited by a young French friend to share a studio in Paris and the result was a two-year stay that was to prove a crucial experience, concluding in the discovery of her own style. Enrolled in no school, she worked on her own and with other artists, the most important of whom were Alfred Pellan and the sculptor Sania Rabinovitch who introduced her to a method of drawing that led to a series of *Dessins analytiques*.

The notebooks Margo Veillon kept during this era, which documented the process of discovery, were unfortunately later destroyed. The series of drawings, however, survived. When they were exhibited in Zurich in 1933, they attracted the attention of the art historian and critic, Doris Wild Gaumann, who became a life-long friend: Doris Wild's last publication was an unfinished contribution to the retrospective volume *Margo Veillon: Une Vie – Une Oeuvre – Une Passion* (Beirut, 1987).

Returning to Egypt in 1932, Margo Veillon was now able to put the assurance she had learned from the *Dessins analytiques* behind her and take up a new task which was to occupy her intermittently for the next 25 years: capturing the verve and movement of daily life in the bedouin settlements near Ma'adi. In 1934 she met the painter Martin Seidel, who became a close friend. They spent five months together on Ibiza in 1935; and it was with Seidel that she made her first trip to

Upper Egypt and Nubia in 1936, photographing, sketching and painting. This remarkable book is the fruit of that trip and six others made before 1964 when Nubia sank forever beneath the waters of Lake Nasser, behind the new Aswan High Dam.

A German national, Seidel, had to leave Egypt at the outbreak of war in 1939. That year, however, she met the American scientist Claude Heman Barlow, war-time head of the American Navy Medical Research Unit in Cairo, who introduced her to the desert. Despite fuel shortages and travel restrictions, they made frequent excursions, often camping out for two or three weeks at a time, during which Margo learned everything she could about desert flora and fauna and assembled her own remarkable geological collection. Until his departure in 1959 they were close companions.

It was not until January and February of 1947 – the year her mother died – that she was able to make her second visit to Nubia, this time accompanied by the painter Suzie Viterbos, with whom she also spent two summers painting at Sant' Angelo Lodigiano and San Colombano al Lambro in Lombardy. In 1950, and again in 1955, she and Suzie Viterbos made two more trips to Nubia, spending a month each time on a ramshackle *dahabiyyah* anchored in the old port of Aswan. These sojourns are recorded in daily diaries for the years between 1950 and 1955. In 1956, a year that signalled the end of many foreign communities in Egypt, Suzie Viterbos left the country forever. The following year, however, Margo Veillon was able to go to Nubia again, taking Flörli Steiger – another Humm cousin from Zurich – and the photographer Elie Zalka with her.

That year also marked the beginning of the High Dam project, which would result in the drowning of Nubia and every human artifact it contained, except a dozen or so pharaonic monuments. In March 1960 UNESCO announced a world-wide campaign to save the ancient monuments, including Abu Simbel, but nothing could be done to rescue the living culture of the Nubians themselves. Towards the end of that year Margo Veillon, therefore, spent sixteen days cruising the Nubian Nile with Elie Zalka and Ruth Reichstein, gifted daughter of the 1950 Nobel prize-winner in medicine. Urged on by the fact that everything they were seeing would soon vanish, the three voyagers mounted an ambitious expedition using two boats and conscientiously tried to register as much visual sensation as they could.

A Nubian Ethnographical Survey was finally launched in 1961 with the aim of salvaging at least some record of life in old Nubia; and in 1962, as the dam rose higher, Margo Veillon made two trips with the Swiss photographer, Georg Gerster, who had been commissioned by the Ethnographical Survey to assemble a photographic record. In mid-January Margo Veillon and Georg Gerster flew with the ethnographer Robert Fuerea and the naturalist Annie Gismann to Khartoum. For the next six weeks they travelled the length of Sudanese Nubia, driving by car from village to village, all the way north to Wadi Halfa, cruising and photographing – and in Margo's case, sketching, drawing and painting as well – every day.

The richness of Margo Veillon's life and work cannot begin to be explored here. This book represents only a portion of the impact made upon a superbly able, acute and receptive artist by one of the world's most visually oriented cultures: it thus offers us not only a subject captured at a particular moment in time, which will never be seen again, but the sensitivity and skill of brain, eye and hand that made that capture possible. We are fortunate in having it.

John Rodenbeck
Cairo, 1994

Letter to Doris
30 April 1960

* Doris Wild, the Swiss art historian and a close friend of Margo's.

My dear Doris,*

I have just spent two days clearing my studio after returning from my travels. Within all the chaos of travelling, it is essential that my eyes remain alert and able to take in everything I see around me. Problems in painting abound, and yet, in spite of everything, painting actually *happens* – before you, you have the subjects, the 'phenomena', the visions; they are outside of you and you receive them, absorb them; then, somehow, the work, the transposition happens despite the fatigue, hordes of mosquitoes, and (what I find particularly wearing) all the horrible little complications and misunderstandings with people around you. Fortunately, memory allows for the occasional clean sweep, leaving you fresh and receptive to new sensations.

Nubia, a land condemned to die, offers itself to our view from the boat that we have been on for twelve days so far. Before us lies a sequence of dry, harsh ripples in the desert sand and black mountains. The houses built upon this land are a perfect style, totally adapted to their surroundings and with a rich variety of decoration on their windows and facades. One could spend forever studying these designs and learn more than one would ever need to know about ornament.

I do not know how to begin telling you about the interiors of these houses. All of nature's jewels seem to be there in an extraordinary display; everything is so expressive. There is nothing as beautiful and so in harmony.

But beautiful though things are, life in these villages is like being exiled by the gods – the women are there sometimes for two or three years without their husbands. They are smiling but can become quite hysterical, excluded from the normal life that we know.

And yet what beauty lies in the tiny, fierce orange grains sparkling in the hot sand and in the huge, strangely shaped stones. And further, beyond the banks of the Nile lurks the great desert . . .

A feeling of anxiety takes hold of you when you see things of such outstanding beauty. You become conscious of the artist's obsession to eternalize and feel the need to put all that you see down on canvas or paper. Occasionally, and this is almost painfully beautiful to witness, the Nile becomes a long, flat mirror; the reflection upon its surface has a completely abstract quality and the light on the water reflecting the sky is extraordinary. One single ripple will carry streaks of an intense cobalt blue and of yellow – or rather gold, bronze or creamy yellow – all sparkling with lilac and mauve. From time to time in this seemingly flat landscape there will appear a black mountain enveloped in sand.

According to the level of the water, the small islands resting on the Nile will disappear and reappear. The river is running high at the moment, so these stretches of plantation are all submerged in water. There is an enormous variety of birds on this stretch of water: pelicans, ibises, herons, wild ducks and swans. My God, if only the world could be created over again with creatures other than cruel human beings.

Apart from the beauty revealed in the landscape unfurling before one's eyes, I have also to mention the beauty of Nubian women. Their jewellery is so beautifully arranged around their necks while their faces are framed within a thick black double set of earrings, which they all wear. Their beauty, however, can only be witnessed fleetingly as they tend to hide in their homes, coming out on occasion and giggling childishly. Their voices seem to sing yet they are shrill.

Everything appears to be in harmony here; it all follows the same rhythm; and artifice has not spoilt anything as it has with city-dwellers. So everything is presented in its pure form and each element becomes a pictorial 'source' for me.

Recently we went by chance to a village and to the house of the chauffeur of Dr Naumare, a professor at the American University. He was a perfect gentleman, extremely hospitable and made us feel completely at ease in his home. He showed us the various rooms in his house, each more beautiful than the one before, and each one exquisitely decorated. Walls were painted and adorned with an array of baskets, rugs, paper cuttings, all of varied symmetry.

In other villages I have been to, each one having its own particular way of ornamentation, I have seen rooms decorated with little plates made of packets of cigarettes, and newspapers transformed into rugs. The overall effect is stunning. On a wall in the square of one of the villages a young girl had cut out in sheets of varied coloured plastic material a series of people and animals. I saw this one morning. I was completely taken aback by this display of colours and decorative instinct. The material the girl had used gave a surprisingly impressive result – surfaces of colour that seemed to be dancing on the stillness of the dark grey wall.

I hardly looked at the temple at Abu Simbel . . . I couldn't take my eyes away from the landscape around it. The day after visiting Abu Simbel we went for a long walk on the mountain. So many colours and so many contrasts in colour were revealed to me there: violet, green shades or red and yellow of a multitude of depth and densities.

The Nile today is very still and dark. Where there is a mist floating upon the water soft shades of green bring the river to life. It is wonderful to sit and watch the water as the mist lifts off and drifts away. I was in the middle of putting this perfect landscape onto paper one day when I noticed a group of Nubian children nearby laughing heartily, their frizzy hair blowing in all directions in the wind. They stayed for only a very short while – a fleeting moment in the diminishing light of day. Which brings to mind the group of women I saw not so long ago in the village of Korosko – three women in black wearing turquoise blue veils standing against a white wall; again seen in the dimness after sunset . . .

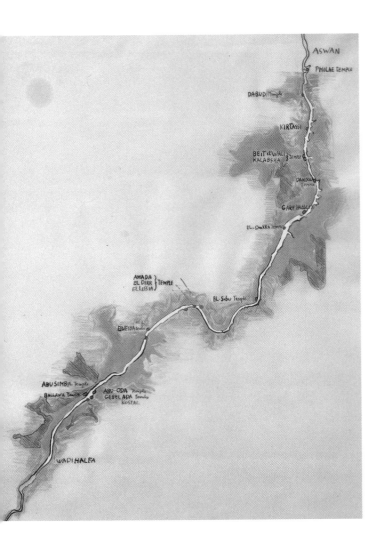

Aswan Diary 1950

Suzy and I are staying on a *dahabiyyah*;* this will be our floating home throughout our time here in Nubia.

Today, **Saturday the 27th**, I begin work on a striking scene: ten or so children who are helping with the unloading of water-jugs.

Everyone passes by especially to greet and welcome us to their land, including Governor Boutros.

Our lifestyle will be primitive on this boat, but to us it seems like paradise after two very trying days. However, the narrow staircase does require an elaborate Chaplinesque routine to climb.

Equipment is passed aboard, people telling us that while we are here they are at our disposal.

My subject for the afternoon is the dom palm grove. The mountains in the background are red. I'm working on the Nubian village with its view of the long white wall and the cupolas; their painting is explicit and varied. I watch the blind man and his wife pass by; he puts down his stick and takes off his shoes to rest and his wife gives him a drink. He stretches out and immediately falls asleep and begins to snore.

Yesterday, Friday – The day was wasted thanks to my migraine. I begin a sketch of the boats that are being

* *Dahabiyyah* is a wooden houseboat.

repaired, but night unfortunately descends quickly and so I have to stop.

Thursday, 25th October – We spend the morning at Souk al Khamis (the Thursday market) where I work on a scene of women under their parasols selling chickens, oranges, dates and palm leaves. The evening was spent tidying our *dahabiyyah*.

Sunday – Ibrahim has a bad cold. Abdel Rahman has injured his leg on a girder. Suzy has lost a filling and I have a toothache. We ate at the Boutros's who gave us more than enough to gorge ourselves on. I feel absolutely bloated – hospitality can be most insistent!

The meal included noodles, salad, meatballs, stuffed courgettes, turkey stuffed with rice and liver, ladies' fingers, stewed pear, and Coca-Cola followed by pudding. They even gave us cake to take home with us!

Monday – This morning I work on the view from my window, with the boats in the foreground and yellow mountains beyond.

Tuesday morning – We stay put and I study the boats and their little pink and brick-coloured pots.

We go out later in the evening. Suzy finds some beautiful plates made of woven reeds.

Yesterday, Wednesday 1st November – In the Gharb Aswan we see the famous Nubian interiors which are completely decorated with reeds. The designs are charming, all geometric patterns and bright colours. On the ceiling there are around fifty baskets all packed together with plaited reeds.

One of the girls at the village, called Raisa, befriends Suzy and me: she calls us Zouzou and Margu.

On the canopy in one of the bedrooms, we saw an incredible array of coloured handkerchiefs tied together on a string giving a joyful note to the room. You could make twenty dresses from this printed material, enough for years to come.

Suzy and I gazed at the yellow mountains opposite and watched the Sahel coming to life around us. Here, the loading and unloading of the cargo boats takes place and every day we witness something new and different; sometimes it is a café with a reed wall, or a group of men will finish the construction of a boat which has the appearance of a black skeleton, having done everything by hand and cut the wood themselves. The fishermen and tradesmen are all bustling about, while the Nile lies serenely before us, sometimes blue, at other times a muddy shade of beige and often reflecting amazing yellow glints from the large hill opposite, shot with a line of intense blue which then turns into a lighter shade before eventually fading from view.

Every day each discovery adds to all the others we have made: the Nubian village with its long courtyards and arches; on the white walls their painting is astonishing in its composition. Matisse's famous theories of colour are proven here, and the work is even more beautiful in its pure oblivion of any 'theory of art'.

We come across a group of women in black, shouting raucously and screaming piercingly. Some of them are amusing to watch with their exaggerated but comic gestures and grating talk. The jewellery they wear is rich – they have two earrings in each lobe, a solid gold necklace, and around them are swathed heavily embroidered veils of wool and pearls.

Yesterday, on Wednesday afternoon, we were on Elephantine Island. I painted the village near the ruins with the desert and the palm trees in the background.

Thursday – I do a sketch of Sorti, the girl at the market selling chickens and hens. The place comes alive with crowds of women coming here by boat for their morning shopping.

Friday – at Sahel the young girls with their red dresses stand out amongst an orgy of the yellow of the reeds and the blue of the water.

Saturday – I am not in a good mood today and worry about my work and spoil the large canvas in the afternoon. I find a miniature version of the large black rock; this one weighs only five kilos! these rocks are natural sculptures.

Sunday – Early in the morning I work on the rock in the water which reflects the yellow mountain beyond. I do a quick sketch from the *dahabiyyah* and a sketch of my room. In the afternoon I begin the large canvas of the black rock.

Monday – We are on our way to Mahatta. Sailing by, we pass little islands – huge heaps of polished basalt. The rocks are incredibly smooth and look like still, hard versions of the Nubians' bodies.

They are eroded, grooved, lined and contorted – all very evocative in shape. This climate seems favourable to the moulding of hard stones of every shape and size. The combination of grey sand and silt, the tiny plants, the striations in the earth and the rocks and yellow desert sand in the distance is sublime.

The village of Mahatta has lost its former charm and the houses are in ruins. However, the position of the village and the composition of the Nubian houses are in harmony with the rocky surrounding. We take tea with the Nubians. These people for the most part are wise enough to maintain their own character which makes me like them very much.

Their love of decoration is wonderful. It is unique

and imitates nothing. Fortunately, they have not yet been influenced by the obsession for the 'modern' as so many others have.

From the top of a rock where I am working on my fourth drawing, I can see Suzy below dancing with a huge group of children before the rocks.

Our Aswan journey is truly satisfying but there is one thing that annoys me about it and that is a certain type of person who comes from a town; in groups, they stare impertinently and do nothing but insult, jeer and make an exhibition of themselves. It is so sad to see this in a country whose beauty is unimaginable.

It seems as if these people are not aware of what beauty they are surrounded by, for it has no effect on them, and they behave in an appalling manner.

At Gharb Aswan we discover folkloric objects.

We spend **Wednesday** at a small Nubian village. At the school the little girls are in dresses with Matisse-like prints on them. The boys wear their *ta'iyya* which are exquisitely embroidered. The teacher seems awful.

Later we see the baskets at Raisa's which are all named, such as: half the world, girl's heads, flower, king and queen, cockroach.

Thursday was spent at the souk again. Nothing of particular interest happened whilst we were there but on the way back we had the opportunity to feast our eyes on the boats on the Nile, watching them loading their cargo. Their sails were at half-mast catching all kinds of light of the early afternoon. We see groups of women in black and girls wrapped in bright colours carrying their gaudy baskets.

All these multifarious shapes and colours contrast with the long black and white robes that the men wear which brings the group together in one solid mass, strengthening its uniformity.

The rocks are like the soul's subconscious stream, while the currents, still water, shadows and reflections, play games within the subconscious flow.

Friday – A day devoted to painting the rocks and studying the varying purplish-blue shades higher upon the slopes and the redder shades lower down.

The immaculate polished black of the rocks reflects the sky, and the glimmers play within their grooves and on their smooth rounded forms. For me, one main problem is the setting of these natural monuments: the rocks surrounded by a pool of water seem more in harmony with the water they are in, which reflects its shining surface, rather than the rocks which sit upon the severe lines of the undulating desert sand.

Saturday 11th November – It is very early, just before sunrise. I am looking at Sahel and thinking about its colours that I love more and more as time passes.

We find ourselves facing the large rock, so black and smooth it directly reflects the sky. This is a beautiful scene which I should like to work on on my next visit to Aswan.

This evening we took a man who had fallen ill to the other side of the river.

Sunday – We are very tired today . . . Anyway, we still go and work at the rock, both in the morning and afternoon. The resulting oil is ill-fated – I haven't 'touched the essence' the sketches had appeared to promise.

Our last day here, **Monday 13th** – There is a very strong wind today. We say goodbye to the villagers and go to the home of two newly-weds. It was extraordinary . . . Everything in the room is pure Nubian; it contained the girl's trousseau: many geometrically-patterned baskets and a solid gold plate. I do a sketch of a chest which is beautifully designed with bright, primary colours.

The colours used in the paintings that I have seen on the white walls here leave a strong impression. By contrast, the women dressed in black merge with the shadows of the night. Meanwhile, the sails of the boats on the Nile, seen together with their reflections on the water, look like huge white butterflies flitting in the black of the night.

We leave our *dahabiyyah* today, having packed 32 boxes of things.

The women selling their wares beneath the black arch of the Sheikh's tomb at the Souk el Khamis transform it into a riot of colour.

Comparing the 'art' of children and madmen and that of logical rational man:

The disinterested, unbiased way the child has of drawing and his joy of playing with lines and colour is, in itself, artistic expression. Disinterestedness signifies complete lack of sentimental expression and imitation of what he sees. The impartiality of the adult losing himself in artistic expression is an achievement in the sense that he breaks loose from convention, mannerism, fashion, and any other sort of artistic malady, in order to arrive at the heart of a thing.

19

21

23

les portes

26

la belle fille de Selnah qui peint
tout les oiseaux et décor ce village

28

un crépuscule d'une beauté inouï

Notre habitation

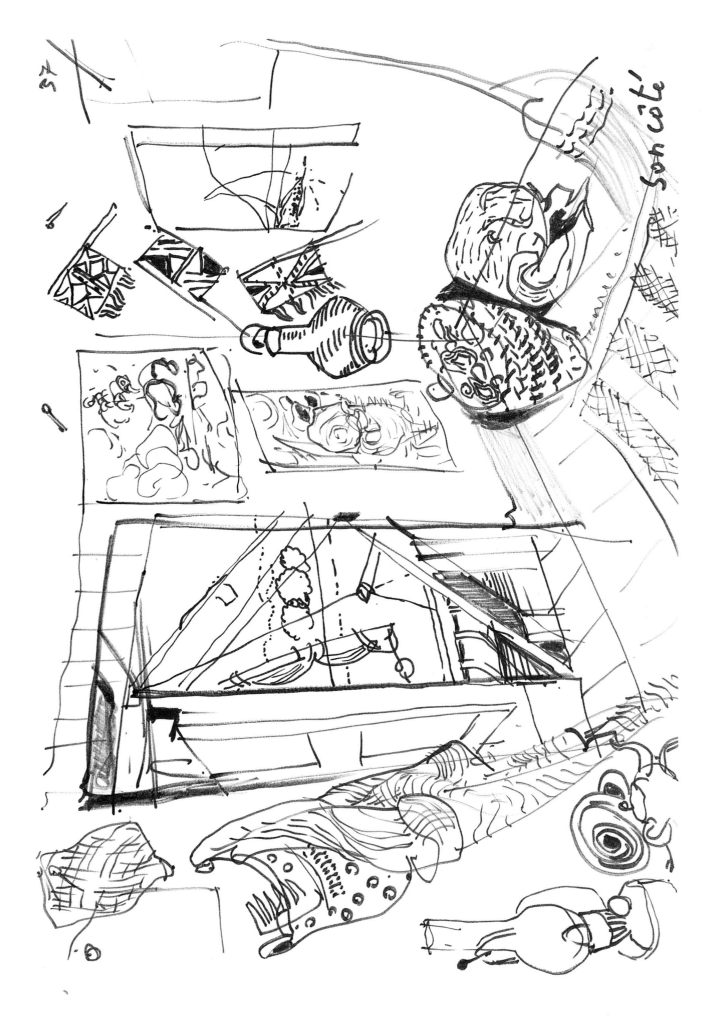

la barque qu'ils essayent
de démarrer

7

démarrage d'une feloucka

toutes les fissures du bâteau sont bourré de
fibres du palmier passé au goudron.

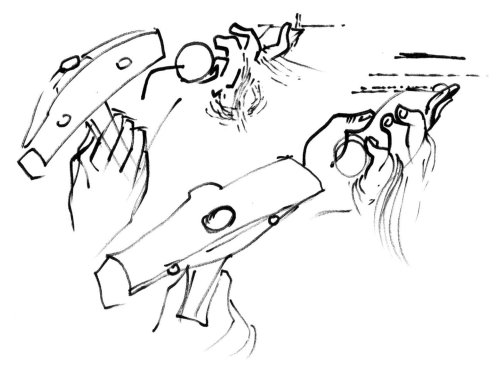

Susy me passe la foulah puis me dit de remettre le mur a sa place.

Hier nous avons fait une visite "Bizou" chez la tante charmante Mme Boutros qui avait en visite deux madames dont une nous causa sans répit de son chien loulou s'appelant "Bijou" qu'elle emmit fil a chaute vctfil lic susta pour le passy à l'oeil dans le train, la femme du commissaire. Susy pique plusieurs

47

crise de fou-rire et jongle avec sa tasse de chocolat et la chute des biscuits - Je n'ose trop la regarder de peur de la contagion - Néanmoins nous sortant asez digne avec beaucoup de salamato.

le tout avoumle est intéressé, Boutros doit nous aider a nous faire passer tout notre bagages qui journellement augmente. les agates, les dattes, les rochers en basalt, etc.

Lundi - Sur l'île au bas du Sh. At. le matin tôt m'installe sur le rocher au reflet bleu prune mirotant ou bronze clair en forme plastique et tout lisse. - après-midi commence grande toile des rochers dans l'eau avec le fond de dunes.

Vendredi au Sahel ; Chargement de charette avec la "cruis" ou la "rivière rouge"

les ptites filles avec leurs robes rouges roses carmin jaune ; l'orgie des jaunes et des tout salir parmi et de des couleurs frilles bruns leurs détails de l'univers minéral leurs bruns des

le marché

le charetier prend son bain
la roue roule quand même

Reminiscence II

les femmes bondement affifées de leurs robes
voli brodé on bordé epriblent leur héâte
à ortant d'une floffte richement décorés.

les invitées quittent les cieux. —

la main henné.

56

58

59

le frisson crispe   Tancrède Villon

la petite avec le grand séjour un
marpeillon argent.

72

73

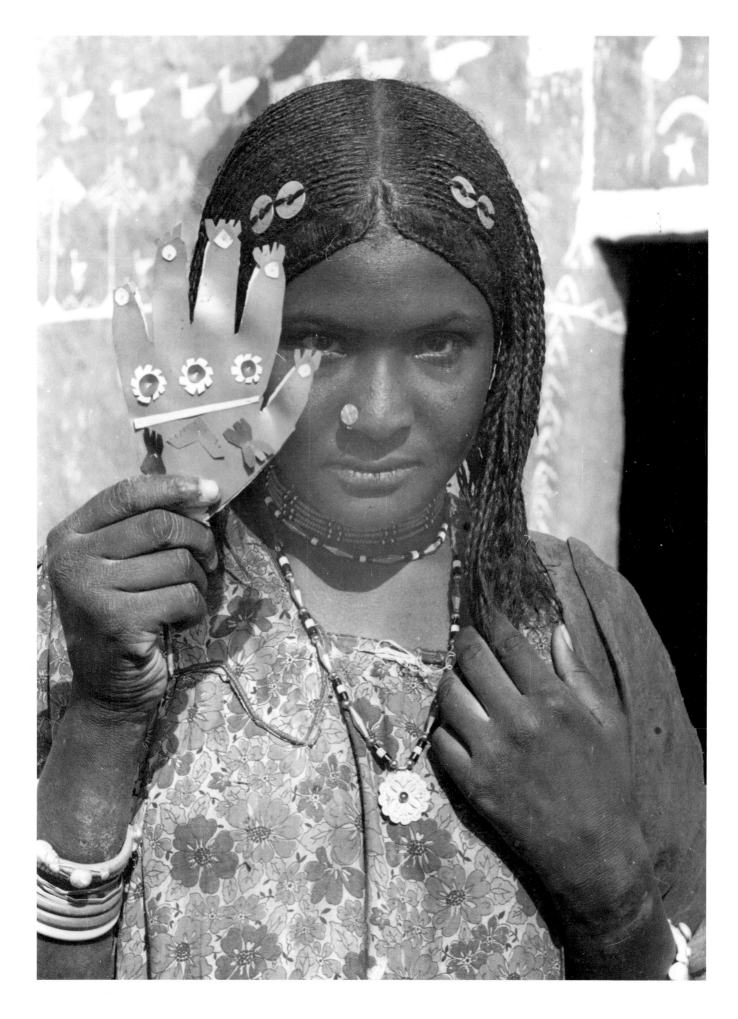

Aswan 1955
24th November to 17th December

Friday, Saturday, Sunday and Monday – Today I shall begin my journal of the days spent here. Suzy and I are staying on the *dahabiyyah* again, together with Abdel Rahman, the old watchman, Abdu 'the grumbler', our cook, and Eleisha our boatman. One nice surprise today is seeing the decoration on the doorway at Taha's house – a drawing of a vulture with a dove's head. I buy three brightly coloured *ta'iyya* (caps) which are decorated with geometric patterns.

Unfortunately the screams and shouts of the women and their children prevent us from working in the afternoon, ruining our concentration.

Our first night here the moon sheds its light onto the whole landscape and the basalt rocks. We contemplate the beauty of this ancient place and in the rocks rediscover Adam and Eve.

I spend **Sunday** morning painting from the *dahabiyyah*, at the golden hour just when the sun rises. The result on the canvas, however, is not as golden. Later in the afternoon we go for a walk to the 'Adam and Eve' group of rocks.

When we had seen them on Saturday night in the moonlight they looked even more fantastic. Our strolls at night are magnificent. The huge shapes are simplified and the rocky mass is an overwhelming sight to behold.

We find a mound of agate, Suzy shrieks with delight at our discovery. I walk closely behind her as we rummage through the stones.

On **Friday**, the day of our arrival, we managed around noon to finish fitting out the boat, throwing out 16 chairs and 2 tables, one of which was absolutely dreadful. At the market at Aswan we buy baskets, fabrics and fans. Everything looks lovely from the window with its view of the incredibly orange hill and the Nile with its sometimes smooth surface with tiny blue ripples and the yellow reflection from the mountains. The boats on the water go from golden to bronze to a purplish-blue depending on the time of the day. On Saturday afternoon we visited Sahel; I find the pottery there delightful – one motif is constantly repeated from every angle resulting in a beautiful decorative pattern.

The women are beautiful with their heaps of jewellery framing their faces and adorning their bodies: their double earrings – two earrings on each lobe – their gold necklaces of a chain of gold squares, and a longer necklace with a large medallion hanging from it. But

their voices are really quite unbearable! Well, all except for Taha's wife who is as refined and well mannered as he is. We see the same faces again as those of five years ago. Raisa, for instance, who was so beautiful then, still has the same lovely look; she greets us politely but she is already worn out even at this young age.

I notice a drawing of a dancing horse on the large doorway of the village.

Tuesday begins with windy weather; a local tells us that it is the devil blowing on us. There seem to be a few boats mooring today as the Nile is quite rough.

'I don't want to disturb the statue,' says Suzy catching me unawares in the middle of my meditation on the failure of all my paintings up till now. She adds that if I carry on looking like this I shall turn into Amenophis III. Her witticism unfortunately cannot change my dismay at my painting catastrophe.

After that, the statue rises to attend the ritual passage of Sitti Zouzou, who is suffering from lumbago.

Outside, the moonlight sheds its light upon the landscape, and I can hear the wind whistling and groaning.

Wednesday – Our day begins at 5 o'clock while the full moon is still above the mountains. The night sky is spread out above; but a touch of morning is beginning to warm the orange land. I wanted to do a quick sketch of this but, thanks to all the mess in the room, I fail to have my material ready in time to capture the moment. Today, both of us are tackling a large canvas each of the row of moored *feluccas* – I myself painting a view from my room. Yesterday evening the boats were flooded with the colours of twilight – shades of dusky sky streaked with orange clouds. We painted till 10 o'clock then continued our morning at the basalt rocks – Adam and Eve's group – where I began working on the large canvas.

Thursday, 1st December – A rather eventful day due to our trip to the bustling, noisy market. It's so colourful too, and entertaining to watch the women selling their mats and baskets.

Abdel Rahman tells us how proud he is of his age. He claims he is a hundred and twenty-five years old!

Friday, 2nd December – I attempt an oil painting from the boat: reflections on the water – the same theme as yesterday evening. But instead of the violet and orange dominating the canvas as I had wanted, I come out with a mauvey-pink and turquoise green.

On the way to the rocks I come across the fisherman's red boat. Its nets are spread out like wings all around it, and the black rocks are slumbering in the background. Groups of boats are dotted about the river, and I can hear the sound of men's laughter drifting from them to where I am walking.

I am now at the rock – my second session on the large canvas. Aswan is beginning to fill up with crowds of town-dwellers and Europeanised Nubian school children. I can't say that I like this intrusion, and there is not a single boat passing by which doesn't have someone making a tasteless or stupid comment. But I shan't allow myself to be upset by this unfortunate clash between the silence of the rock and the wretched men who pass by in their boats arguing and grumbling continuously.

We return at 2 o'clock – on the way back we take a little time to search for agates. At twilight I do a study for a lithograph using the *feluccas* as a pattern.

Saturday – Early this morning we try to paint the morning colours of the hill opposite; its colours differ every day. Today, it is mauve with traces of pale violet on the orange sand; as the morning progressively heats up, its colour becomes more intense in the sunlight; while yesterday, a veil of translucent carmine covered the golden sand. In the evening, with the light shining from behind the sand, the undulating dunes in shades of raw sienna merge with a rosy naples yellow. The most dazzling is the orangey-red which shimmers in an extraordinary way when the trails of cobalt blue in the water cut across the line of gleaming yellow.

Our *felucca* takes us to a village in the Gharb Aswan called Bassion. There we are welcomed by Abdel Raszeh. The village is surrounded by beautiful vegetation and is built against hills of dark yellow dunes. The people here are very friendly and hospitable, welcoming us into their homes. It is incredible how in the various rooms of the

houses each object becomes a decorative element. Even the cutlery placed on the shelves is a pretext for decoration. There are some extremely beautiful flat baskets – the 'Kubri Zamalek', for example – but they do not want to sell them. All along the walls, right up to the ceiling, there are arranged plates, handkerchiefs, fabric and baskets, all in a symmetrical pattern. The back wall is decorated with baskets with geometric designs, some figures and a *tarn* with writing from the Koran. I discovered one new ornamental motif: coloured paper birds attached to the surface of the ceiling, always in pairs as a mating symbol.

Sunday – A cold wind is blowing today. I take my 5 o'clock tea and excitedly work on a quick sketch in an attempt to catch the fleeting colours of the morning. However, it is a grey day. I walk to Sahel taking my sketch pad with me, and two rather well-dressed men shout out a vulgar *bint el kelb* as they pass by. By contrast, the boatmen and traders each have a funny or nice word to say. At Sahel I see many people carrying pots; all of them are wonderfully coloured in dark, earthy red, and yellow.

Ingrid, Bettula, Korgossa, Amné, Harun, Kullia, Dadda, Daia, Alle . . . a few Nubian girls' names.

We pass the men working on the boats; they are filling them with palm matting that has been smeared with tar thus finishing off the structural work on the *felucca*.

Around 11 o'clock at the village we come across a room that is not as full as the other typical Bassion rooms, but interesting nevertheless. We see many more names displayed on the baskets: *Kubri Zamalek, Muski, Mahgara, Ginen el Hananel*. A young girl is drawing a pretty picture on the wall. Later, I begin a study of these in oil.

I work on a picture of a handsome black man wearing a yellow waistcoat. His skin shines like the basalt rock. His turban is twisted round six times, and his *galabiyyah* is blue.

Monday – It is cold and windy and outside everything is a dull grey. I have been at the rock from 9.30 until 3.30 – my third time on the large canvas. At around 1.30 I begin the landscape from the top of the island.

Tuesday, 6th December – I'm slightly irritated by Eleisha who seems to take ages to do anything . . .

We went to the island opposite Mahatta. The landscape there is wonderful; basalt rocks are

Diary continues on page 87

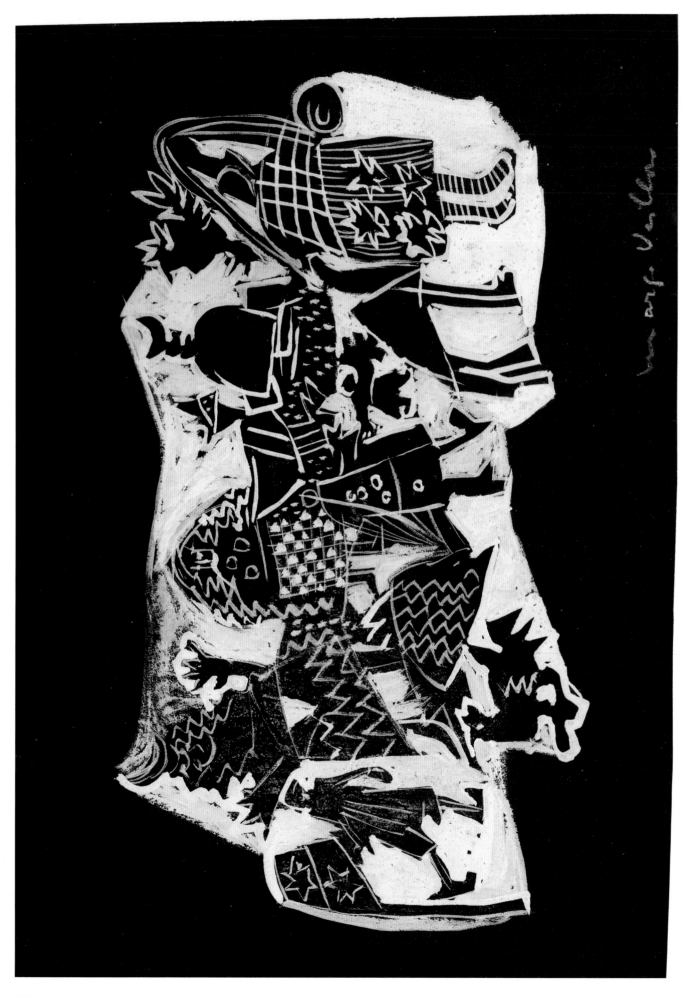

86

Some Neapolitans – luckily before the spectacle of the accident – shout out greetings to us as well as a few of the *romantico sympatico* type of comments. I have to add that I would rather hear that than an offensive *bint el kelb*!

The really tiring part of the day is having to pack and unpack all our material which includes my box, her box, the camera, bottles, a satchel of paints, sketchpads, etc, parasols, a chair each, our portfolios, food, and at least four or five large canvases. We seem to be coming and going with them continuously; it is not surprising that Eleisha always has that dissatisfied look on his face.

However, worst of all is having to clean twenty or more brushes and the rest of my things later in the day, while I can see my nightdress on the other side of the room that I am longing to get into. And yet, my greatest satisfaction lies in painting, and I would rather face these exhausting tasks than be deprived of this rich and wonderful landscape.

Friday – We return to Sahel. Today was an exceptionally colourful day. We later stop near Sheikh Atman's tomb so that we can rummage through the heaps of basalt stones. The rocks are an incredibly shiny metallic blue with bronze glints. This moonlike landscape is truly bewildering. I shall have to spend more time on it on my next visit. Later, twilight was just perfect . . .

Saturday – A sunrise with small ribbon-like clouds,

all very varied in colour. I change to oils and work on a quick sketch of our room. Abdel Rahman is ill.

Sunday – It is cold and I am feeling ill. I attempt a drawing of a boat whose mended sail is being hoisted.

Mr Boutros said that he would help us with our luggage, of which more and more is accumulating every day . . . agates, dates, basalt stones, etc.

Monday – On the island below Sheikh Atman I go and sit at the rock very early today. Its prussian blue glints are mirrored in the water. In the afternoon I work on the large canvas of the rocks on the water with the dunes in the background.

Tuesday, 13th – The weather is calm and the Atman Island is prettily reflected in the water. It is my second session on the square canvas. I break some smooth and polished rock into little pieces with a piece of iron.

It is hot, and the heat is making us feel sleepy as we are working. We return around 3.30. From my window at twilight I can see a man in white helping some women dressed in black onto the boat. The black and white look extraordinary in the dim bluish hue of the night.

Mornings from the boat. Elephantine Island landscape.

Wednesday, 14th December – Evening. We witnessed a beautiful sunset on our return from Atman Island.

A beautiful day: it is hot and there is no wind. I work on a study for a lithograph in the morning of the reflections, while the afternoon was spent at Atman Island.

Thursday – The mist of the morning was followed by a pleasant breeze. The boats are returning and it will be wonderful and animated here later on. We were at the village today and all through our visit we were surrounded by screaming, chattering children, who were later joined by more people – men, as well as women – all making such a racket! My ears are still ringing this evening from all the noise and shrill voices.

We did not manage a minute's peace during our work. The sunset, as we made our way back to our *dahabiyyah* was wonderful with traces of clouds that remained in the sky for a long while, right up until total darkness set in.

Our last day at Gharb Aswan. A decorated wall.

Our departure. We left with 26 boxes of things! My final view of Gharb Aswan was of the sails grouped together before the hill. Light against darkness – then it became a silhouette against the sky, adorned with shades of orange and pink, upon glistening pools of water . . .

ASSUAN.

Jeudi – hier on veut à gonfler le diable

mon empêche de continuer mes tableaux commencé

quelque à midi, avant cela un cinéaste américain

mon frère – quelques croquis depuis le bergère, –

en ville etc – puis essai perdre mon calme de

croquis n'en dort pas la nuit. —

Jeudi donc belle aurore, early ? en système

prélude dans la colline de Sheich el Hawa

rose miel ciel sale bergère, "graphographe

puis vers 9½ p.m 5½ am ?¾ –

rencontre la grande Tot enfant elle du lac un air

haut pas. Sury a un peti-machume un

ont de veut lui enchant. Am to es enfant

elle sauve ton un pied sa boîte le pouvant coté

puis nous partons la pêche au tigre.

2

1

Les Napolitains avant cette chute (heureusement
mi de Salutis et entre autre Laura un
romantico sympathico, se qui et grand même
moins qu'un luit d'Italie. —

91

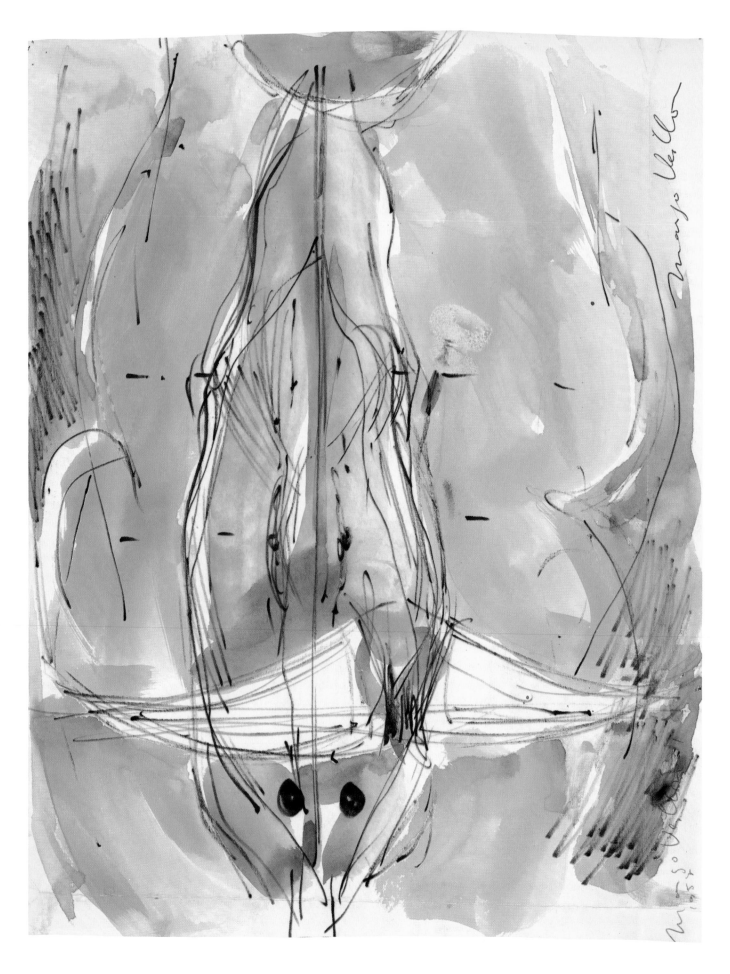

92

93

Les grandes enrées de la fourni ont été
emmagasiné et déménagement du matériel
me rend allègre

ma toile sa boîte   photo   lauteilles   sug phato   croyra cahier   harasse chinant   7+1= 2 deux

cartons

susy

toustfailles   bouget sug

et qui reviens

ils sont des aller et venir

4 en 5 très paul fayance
tous fois
c'est pas
élémement
il Elude à Tryone
une même noir et sombre

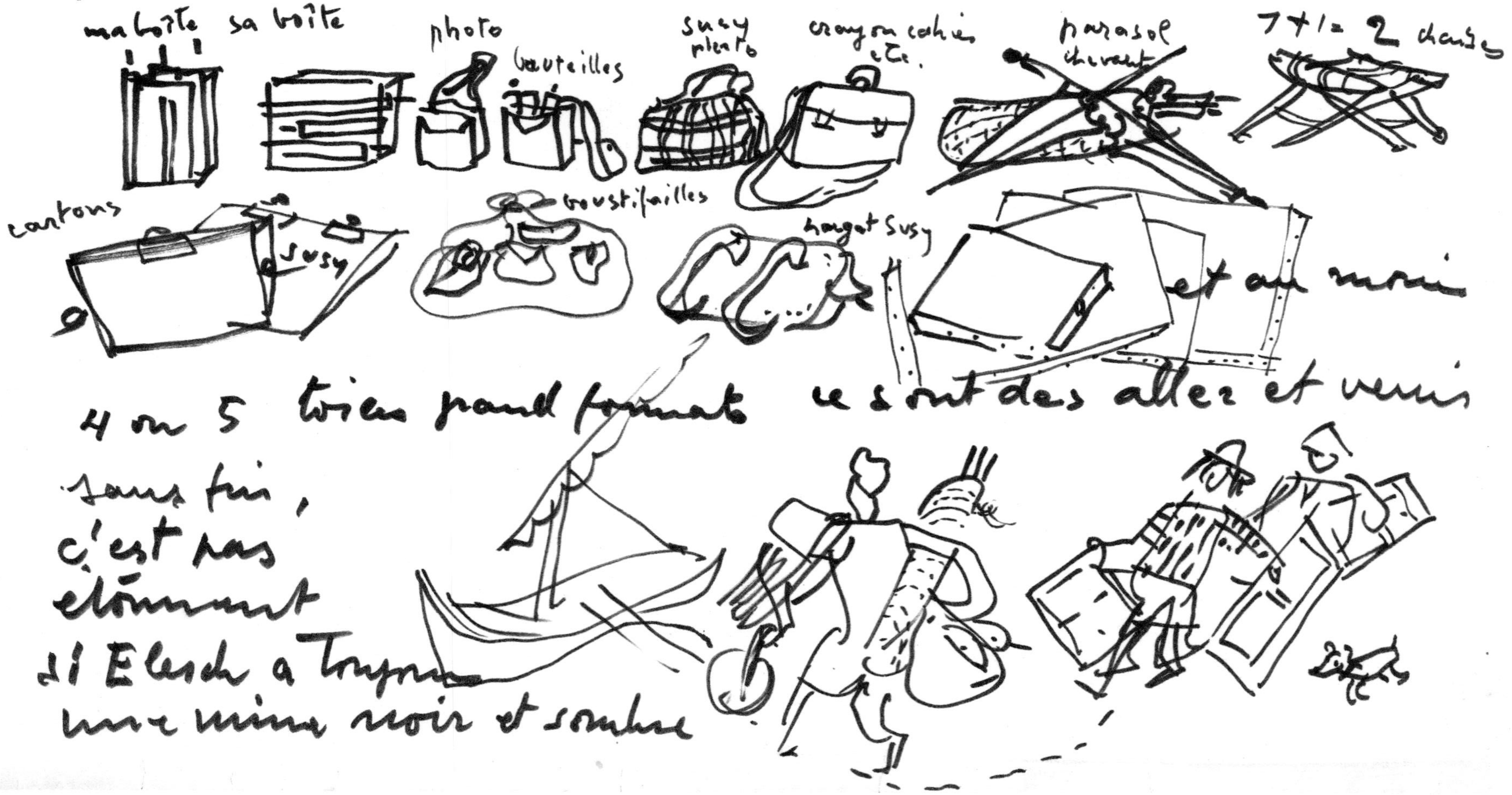

mais bien que tout c'est le nettoyage des 20 pinceaux
en plus et du matériel

mais aucune satisfaction plus grande que peindre.

tandis que m'attend au loin ma cheminée qui cuit

95

101

105

109

110

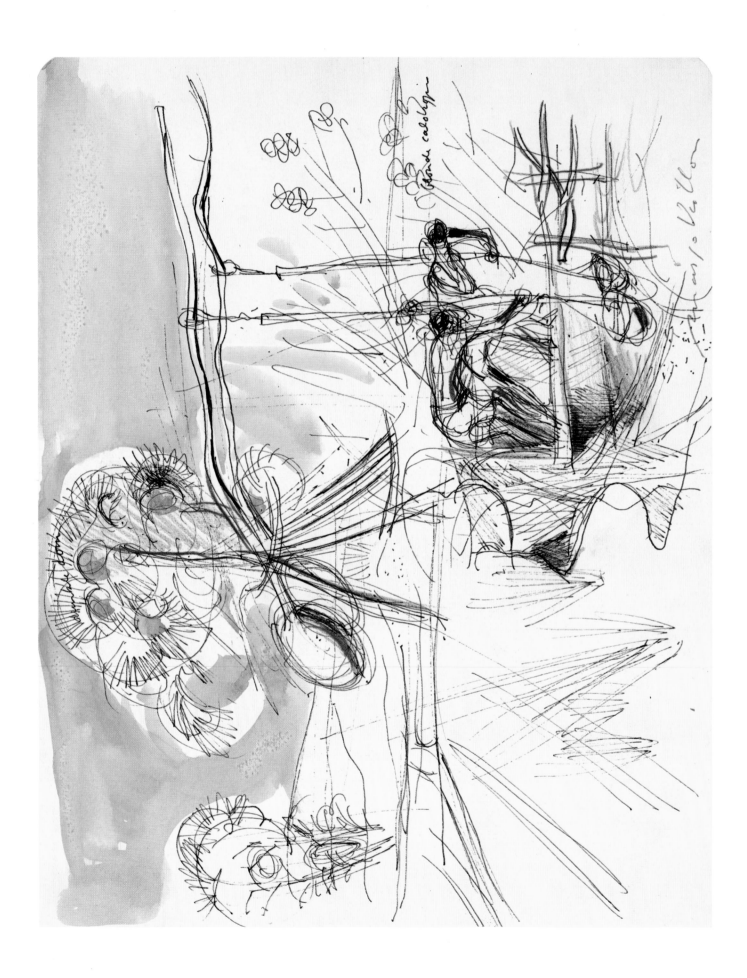

116

Wadi' Halfa   Maya Va Ela   1962

119

123

les tombeaux

Picasso Vallon

la barque a tourné de mois
à Senya et le signal
d'enrouler la voile

128

... leurs peintures primitives explicatives
et fortes de couleurs sur le mur blanc,
les groupes noirs des femmes et les
ombres consolidant le vide de la
grande lumière . . . .

un tableau avec les teintes compliquées de la nature opposés   aux couleurs primaire de l'ôa peinture primitif

les ibis sur le rocher noir et le
fond rose des villages

· réminiscence

ces voiles ressemblaient avec leur reflet a d'énorme papillon blanc, obscurissant
par leur blancheur, ciel et eau. —   39

.. grosse weisse, gelbe -gefleckte gestreifte Segeln
flattern oder in vollen Segel mit
wiederspiegelung
  wie riesen weisse Schmetterlinge
verdunkeln rings um sich wasser u.
luft. ——

130

femme habillée de noir devant
portait terre très jaune

132

acheteurs installons que que tu sois, Susy trouve de
telles assiettes de paiches. —
Hier mercredi le 1 Novembre au village gine assis on
l'intérieur fameux étant décoré de couverle,
en paille avec chacun un autre dessin géométrique
en vé couleurs Sur le plafond une
ainpantaine d'écuell
attaché avec la paille
turné fait leur déc.
conventionnel, tout
est pour le Mausar
Raïsia devient notre
amie et s'appelle "Zouzou
et Marrju
Sur le tit balda puis du lit
une quantité de mouchoirs
coloré donne une note gai
d'œuf de pâques sur une palle
vingt imprimé pour des

mercredi au village berbère. — l'école des
tout petits les fillettes en robe a la Matisse les
garçons avec leur tata a broderie fine, le prof.
odieux, citadin. — Chez Raïsia. les paniers
ont chacun un nom. p. ex.
NUSS ELDUNIA - MARUÄHA - ADAÑI - SAGÄGA - CIMA
ZIRSÉR RUKS ELBANAT - SHÄMI - MENDIL AHMEDABRASCHIDI
MELÉK U MELEKA - WÄRD - TABÄELSUK - BOAÄA ELMULUK

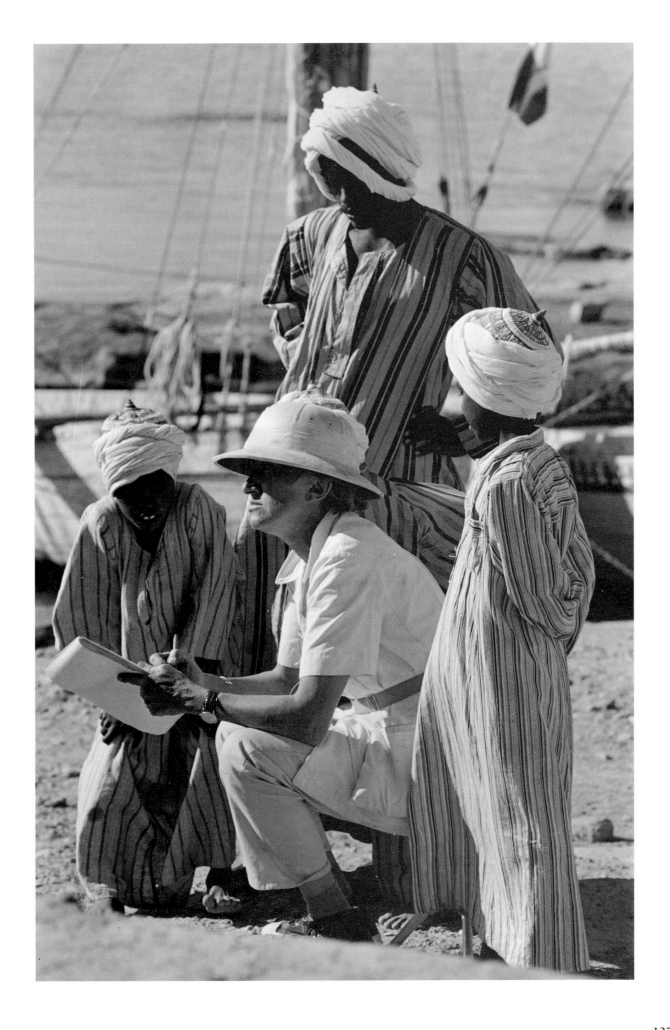

Diary June 1962

We are journeying on the Horia – zigzagging our way along the Nile, the length of Nubia from Shellal to Ballana.

. . . **The following day** we made our way to the temple at Kalabsha and stayed there for a few hours. I felt completely exhausted. These June afternoons the heat is oppressive and in the early evening there is a terribly hot wind, making the Nile look as if it were boiling. The breeze that blows from the desert is stifling, and the only way you can attempt to cool down is by drinking.

We stopped off at a village where we met Sheikh el Balad dressed in blue. He has been Sheikh of this village for twenty-five years.

The roads here are ingeniously widened. The houses with narrow stone staircases snake their way around and up the buildings. The facades of these houses are as in Amsterdam with each door separate yet they are all connected.

This excessive heat is making me feel sick and we do not have the energy to take photographs. I think of Sabria, the little girl I met at the nearby village of Dibtot, her little face and white teeth, bright eyes and laughing voice, all framed within her wiry, frizzy mane.

June 10 – The wind had calmed down today, thank God. We walk to a nearby village and take some photos of the boats and some of the architectural details, including the brickwork in some of the walls which we find out actually serves as a ventilation system. We return to the boat and continue sailing for some time, sweating profusely in the stifling heat.

The highlight of the day was mooring next to one of the dunes. I saw some camomile plants growing in little pockets among the rocks, scorched by the sun. We bathed in the Nile to cool off. We spent the night there, next to the huge body of the dune which was emitting the heat it had gathered in the day. I didn't sleep very well thanks to people talking all through the night. The following day it was even hotter.

On **Monday** we arrived at Gharf Hussein. We spent a few hours there during which I unfortunately felt bored, not having anything to do; Georg meanwhile was working. Around 3 o'clock we headed for the village of Solohé. The women here seemed to be very shy. Indeed, I noticed that they kept hiding from us, pretending to be ashamed of being photographed or painted. I find them rather bourgeois and conventional.

While at the village of Solohé I sketch the marvellous perspective through the arcades of this village. Each one frames a particular scene, while beyond that is the rest of the village, and further beyond the Nile.

We stop for the night near the temple at Kalabsha. There is a madman living here whom we can hear screaming menacingly. His shrieks seem like some kind of grotesque tragedy laughing horribly at 'normality'. I am not going to begin theorising about his situation for it is tragic enough already – he is a simple man; but is it less of a tragedy if this is happening to a simpleton like him rather that someone intelligent gone mad?

Tuesday – the light after Kalabsha was phosphorescent, with sharp oblique shadows cutting their way through the landscape. I watched the women whitewashing the wall with their hands. They still refuse to be photographed.

Later, I continued my study of the arcades which panoramically framed the village. and in the evening we feasted on ice cream.

Wednesday June 20 – I am writing this evening from Hafir, the village with the white mosque that contrasts with the light of dusk.

In the foreground I can see the boats and their sails catching the last rays of warm sun, their ropes and poles forming an intricate grid upon the mosque in the background. I see the men working on the boats – the blues they are wearing go well with the surrounding colours; the background shades are orange which slowly become deep carmine, then deeper still and eventually merge with the colours of the night.

During the day we endured the shouts and grating voices of these quite violent-sounding young women, who behave as if they are jealous of one another. They have their own strict moral code and have a tendency to judge others accordingly. Moreover, they constantly shout above anyone else who is speaking, making a conversation with them impossible.

Their beauty, however, seems to rise above all of this. And yet not only their natural beauty but their ways of making themselves beautiful, for example, plaiting in varied fashion tiny plaits, adding lots of gold-coloured hairpins, pearls, etc.

I worked on the area of Dalonde with its dark violet mountains and dunes, which towards evening turn to gold before the night arrives, while long shadows form, made sharper by the remaining purplish-blue light. The rocks and hills merge into one as darkness descends.

Nubian houses seem like fantastic visions and yet they really do exist. They are superbly thought out – allowing the imagination free rein in their arrangement, and sometimes going beyond the more usual types of decoration.

The Dance – Feast days

There are three dancers. One is in green, the other in stripes and the third in blue. They group themselves around the drummer who is sitting on the floor, playing the drums, a drumstick in each hand. The dancers begin to clap vigorously in time with the music – the clapping of hands is hard and fast. Then they loosen their arms and start clapping in a syncopated rhythm to the drum. The dancer in the striped cloak jumps up, and the others join in, their steps becoming faster and faster and more frenzied.

The Desert and the Valley

One great dune I saw on my visit here gave me the impression of a gigantic mound curiously in transition despite the enormous amount of space that it monopolised. This body of sand, with its sinuous, pointed crest, is truly alive, the rocks and stones nearby seeming to submit to its living presence, which slowly changes the appearance of the landscape. Like a graveyard of small individual mounds adorned with stones on top, the desert near this dune is a field of quartz, and whilst I was there I found an agate as well as several unusual striped rocks. I very much wanted to spend another night here but became weary after all the effort spent in climbing the beautiful dune, and my continual thirst made me return to the boat. As I was leaving, the body of the dune, crouching on large flanks that had been rounded off by the rocky, undulating terrain around it, had taken a new form, looking like a snake coming towards us with unnecessary accumulations of sand having been hollowed out by mutual agreement with the wind. I was drawn back to this transformed mass as it curled up and its back began to approximate to the height of the black mountains which often come near to and wind along the Nile. By now, its sand was a fiery yellow, almost orange in colour.

During the first week of this journey into Nubia, this summer seemed to surpass all others in the number of birds and fish that I saw, particularly the pelicans, and the image of them at Kasr Ibrahim remains one of my most unforgettable memories. They stretched for miles on a sandbar in the river, protected by islands on either side, and seemed determined not to let anything disturb them.

The Nubians themselves seemed occupied with planting wherever they could in order to have a harvest. They did this almost without any tools at all, their hands doing all the work; one woman massaged the muddy ground, breaking up clods of earth and then making sure that it covered the seeds.

The fishermen made nets by threading fishing lines through empty salt tins which served as floats, as well as containers for bait and hooks. With very little effort they were able to close the net and pull in the fish. As the net came closer to the river bank, the large number of fish in each net became more and more disturbed, and began wriggling, jumping and squirming in a frantic effort to escape. As the water became shallower, and they felt the hot air, it seemed as if they all knew they only had a few more minutes to live. The smell of the fish and the mud exalted the area, in this land soon to be covered by the Nile.

Inguiro
Bettula
Korgossa
Ammé
Harun
Kullia
Dadda
Madia
Alle

quelques noms de filles

146

devant la porte bleu

Ce fut une femme
d'usure du temps
elle tient et porte 8 clé
de bois — souples
a honte de sa présence
et veut qu'elle se cache
Elle n'est pas
toute fois impression
ut prétend sa
présence cette
momie vivante
Touchante,
si on la question
sur cette vie
un secret de la
Nubie nous
serg révélé.
la fie de ces
femmes isolés.

148

150

151

deux fauturarujsti epines

152

154

156

157

158

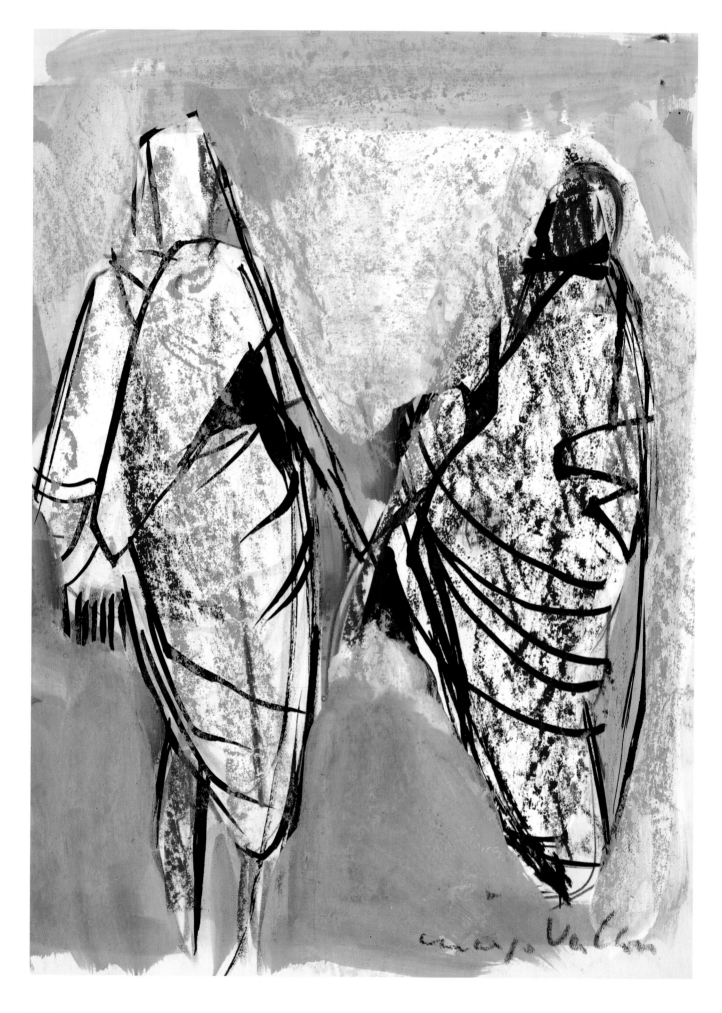

et ça ce fût le commencement. –

32 colis - Départ de la Dahabi

et le départ, 26 colis

88

164

165

Translations of some of the notes accompanying the illustrations are given below:

page 28 Girl from Sebouah who paints all the birds and decorates the village

page 33 Twilight of inexpressible beauty

page 39b All the boat's gaps were caulked with palm-leaf fibres covered in tar.

page 40a Suzy passes me the *goulah* and then tells me to put the wall back in place. Yesterday we paid a visit, 'a *bizour*', to the quite charming Mme Boutros, who was being visited by two ladies, one of whom talked incessantly about her dog Loulou whom she called Jewel. She said – the official's wife – she zipped him up in her bag so she could take him on the train. Susy interjected with . . . .

page 40b . . . attacks of the giggles and juggled with her cup of chocolate and tumbling biscuits. I didn't really dare look at her for fear of catching them. Nevertheless, we left with a fair amount of dignity and with much salaaming.

The result is in our interest: Boutros helped us carry all our luggage which has increased daily, the agates, the dates, the basalt rocks, etc.

Monday – On the island at the bottom of Sh. At., in the morning soon set myself up on the smooth, moulded rock with its sparkling prussian blue and clear bronze highlights.

Afternoon, began the large canvas of rocks in the water with a background of dunes.

page 49 Women dolled up in their black dresses with embroidered borders, passing under a richly decorated doorway.

page 50 Guests leave the feast at Sebouah

page 69 Toddler with a big silver ornament

page 71 Large neutral surface with splashes of colour

page 90 *See* Diary page 87

page 91 *See* Diary page 87

page 94 The great tasks of the day were sorting out and moving the stuff here listed: my box, her box, camera, bottles, Suzy's bag, chalks, books, parasol, windbreak, 1 + 1 = 2 chairs, satchels, grub, Suzy's stuff, and not least four or five large canvases. There are endless comings and goings; it is not surprising Eleisha always has a black and gloomy expression.

page 95 *See* Diary page 87

page 100 . . . hill of black rock, this great dune shifts, descends. Its abrupt pauses are hillocks. Its enormous body takes its shape from the piercing ridge linking line and mass. The dunes are continually in motion. The changing light constantly transforms the shape. Reflections on the dunes.

page 107 Egret flying by an acacia

page 129 . . . their primitive paintings and strength of colours on the white wall, the black groups of women and the shadows reinforced the emptiness and the great light . . .

The ibises on the black rock and the deep rose of the villages.

These sails with their reflections resemble some huge white butterfly, obscuring the sky and water with their whiteness.

[in German] . . . large white, yellow spotted and striped sails fluttering, and a full sail together with its reflection like a huge white butterfly obscuring around itself the water and the air.

page 131 Zigzag woman in black in front of a yellow door

page 136 *See* Diary page 14

page 141 *See* Diary page 16

page 147 In front of the blue door

page 148 There was once a woman. Time takes its toll. She carries eight wooden keys. Her son is ashamed of her and wants her to keep herself concealed. But she's not always afraid and this touching live mummy asserts her presence. If one questioned her, a secret would be revealed – the life of these isolated women.

page 152 Two tambourine players

page 158 Graphic folly that turns into an orgy of colour

List of illustrations